Our Rules

by John Serrano

We have rules.

The rule is "Do your homework."

The rule is "Make the bed."

She makes the bed.

The rule is "Take out the trash."

He takes out the trash.

The rule is "Set the table."

They set the table.

The rule is "Wash the dishes."

They wash the dishes.

The rule is "Wash your hands."

They wash their hands.

The rule is "Wear your seat belt."

They wear seat belts.

We have rules, too.